The Good Nurse

The Real Story of Charles Cullen

Clever James Publishing

Copyright

All rights reserved. No part of this book may be reproduced, stored in a retrieval system, or transmitted in any form or by any means, electronic, mechanical, photocopying, recording, or otherwise, without the prior written permission of the publisher, except for brief quotations used in reviews.

This book is a work of nonfiction. Any similarity to real persons, living or dead, is coincidental and not intended by the author.

© 2024 by Clever James Publishing

Disclaimer

This book, *The Good Nurse: The Real Story of Charles Cullen*, is based on extensive research, including public records, interviews, and media reports. While every effort has been made to accurately represent the events and individuals discussed, certain names, dialogues, and scenes have been modified or reconstructed to preserve privacy and enhance readability. The narrative may include dramatizations for the sake of clarity and flow.

The intent of this book is to provide a factual account of the events surrounding Charles Cullen's crimes, as well as the institutional failures that allowed them to occur. It is not intended to defame, malign, or harm any individuals or organizations, but rather to raise awareness of systemic issues and the importance of accountability within the healthcare system.

Readers are encouraged to consider this work as a blend of documented facts and responsible interpretation, acknowledging that some details may vary due to the passage of time and differing perspectives.

Any similarities to persons, living or deceased, outside of those directly involved in the documented events, are purely coincidental.

Table Of Contents

Introduction.. 6
Chapter One... 15
The Real Story Behind The Deliverance............... 15
Casting and Performances...................................... 23
Chapter Three.. 32
The Filmmaking Process.. 32
Themes and Symbolism..40
Chapter Five...48
Reception and Criticism...48

Introduction

In the quiet halls of hospitals, where trust is the foundation of care, a chilling and unimaginable truth was unfolding. Over the course of 16 years, Charles Cullen, a nurse entrusted with the well-being of his patients, was secretly one of the most prolific serial killers in modern history. He moved from hospital to hospital, undetected by his peers and superiors, leaving behind a trail of unexplained deaths and sorrow. His horrifying actions raised profound questions about the very institutions meant to protect and heal the vulnerable.

This book delves deep into the real story behind the man known as "The Good Nurse," revealing not only the details of Cullen's crimes but also the systemic failures that allowed him to continue his killing spree for so long. It is a story of negligence, deception, and, ultimately, a flawed system that prioritized reputation over patient safety. But at the heart of this tale is also a story of courage—Amy Loughren, a fellow nurse, whose bravery and determination helped bring Cullen's horrific actions to light.

Through extensive research and firsthand accounts, this book uncovers the dark secrets hidden behind hospital walls and the moral and ethical dilemmas faced by those working within the healthcare system. The story of Charles Cullen is more than a recounting of one man's monstrous deeds; it is a reflection of the power of trust, the failures of institutions, and the brave individuals who dare to stand up for what is right, even in the face of unimaginable evil.

Prepare to uncover the truth behind the headlines, as we embark on a journey into the disturbing world of *The Good Nurse*.

Chapter One

Introduction to The Good Nurse

Netflix's "The Good Nurse" brings to life a harrowing story rooted in real-world events, intertwining the chilling tale of one of America's most prolific serial killers, Charles Cullen, with the heroic efforts of a dedicated nurse, Amy Loughren, who ultimately helped bring him to justice. Directed by Tobias Lindholm and starring Academy Award-winning actors Jessica Chastain and Eddie Redmayne, this film is far more than a typical crime drama; it's a powerful exploration of the cracks within the healthcare system that allowed a killer to thrive for so long. The film also underscores the importance of compassion, ethics, and personal bravery in professions where lives are literally at stake.

In the heart of the film is Amy Loughren, a hardworking, compassionate nurse whose dedication to her patients runs deep. Portrayed by Jessica Chastain, Amy is a single mother working long shifts in the ICU of a New Jersey hospital. She is grappling with her own health issues while caring for her children, reflecting the reality of many healthcare workers who often balance the demands of a grueling job with personal challenges. Amy's character is not just a caregiver but someone who embodies the ethical and moral duties that come with the role. Her dedication to her patients makes her a striking contrast to the film's antagonist, Charles Cullen, portrayed with eerie subtlety by Eddie Redmayne.

Charles Cullen, in contrast to Amy's warmth, is depicted as a quiet, seemingly mild-mannered man who slips easily into the fabric of the hospital's night shift. He is calm, even likable, and initially appears to be a good friend to Amy, helping her with work and offering support. However, beneath his helpful demeanor lies a dark secret—Cullen has been killing patients in various hospitals for over a decade, exploiting the trust that is placed in healthcare professionals. The film captures the slow, unnerving realization that Amy comes to as she begins to suspect that her friend and colleague may be behind the mysterious deaths of patients under their care.

The story unfolds with a quiet intensity, reflecting the real-life horror of Cullen's ability to move from one hospital to another, leaving behind a trail of death without consequence. The Good Nurse doesn't rely on overt displays of violence or sensationalism. Instead, it builds tension through the characters' interactions, the subtle shifts in Amy's perception of Cullen, and the creeping dread that grows as more patients inexplicably die. The true horror lies not in graphic depictions of murder but in the system that allowed Cullen to continue killing without intervention. Hospitals, more concerned with avoiding litigation than addressing the real issue, quietly dismissed Cullen rather than report him, allowing him to continue his killing spree across multiple institutions.

As the film progresses, the focus shifts from the crimes themselves to Amy's internal struggle as she pieces together the truth about Cullen. Initially, she is reluctant to believe that someone she has come to trust could be capable of such horrific acts. The bond they share, however tenuous, makes it difficult for her to reconcile the man she knows with the monster he truly is. This emotional conflict is portrayed with remarkable nuance by Chastain, whose performance captures the anguish and disbelief that come with such a revelation. The audience is drawn into Amy's moral quandary, understanding her hesitation while also feeling the urgency of the situation.

Amy's eventual decision to work with law enforcement to expose Cullen is the film's emotional core. It's not just a story of a nurse doing her job; it's a story of moral courage, of a person choosing to do what's right even when it's personally devastating. The weight of this decision is palpable throughout the film. Amy risks her career, her safety, and her friendship to stop Cullen, knowing that the system around her is not designed to protect her or the patients. The filmmakers do an exceptional job of portraying this struggle without melodrama, allowing the gravity of the situation to speak for itself.

Eddie Redmayne's portrayal of Charles Cullen is equally compelling, though in a much quieter, more restrained way. Redmayne gives Cullen a cold, detached persona, making his character's actions all the more disturbing. He is not a typical cinematic villain; there are no grand speeches or overt signs of malice. Instead, Cullen operates in the shadows, committing acts of unimaginable cruelty with an almost indifferent air. This quiet, unassuming manner makes him all the more terrifying because it feels so plausible. The film leaves audiences with the chilling realization that monsters like Cullen can hide in plain sight, cloaked by the trust that comes with their positions.

One of the most striking elements of The Good Nurse is how it handles the theme of systemic failure. The film doesn't just point fingers at Charles Cullen as an individual but also at the institutions that enabled him. The hospitals that employed Cullen were more concerned with protecting their reputations than with the safety of their patients. Time and again, Cullen was quietly dismissed when suspicions arose, with no real effort made to investigate or stop him.

This failure allowed him to move from one hospital to the next, continuing his killing spree. The film raises important questions about accountability and the responsibility of healthcare institutions to protect their patients, even when doing so might expose them to liability.

The tension between personal responsibility and institutional failure is central to the film's message. Amy Loughren's story is one of personal bravery, but it is set against the backdrop of a deeply flawed system that failed at every turn. The film subtly critiques this system, not through heavy-handed exposition but by showing the human cost of these failures. Each patient's death is a tragedy, not just because of Cullen's actions but because it could have been prevented if someone had acted sooner. This makes The Good Nurse not just a crime drama but a sobering look at the consequences of inaction and the ethical responsibilities of those in positions of power.

As the film moves toward its climax, the tension becomes almost unbearable. Amy, now fully aware of Cullen's crimes, works with detectives to gather the evidence needed to stop him. This requires her to continue interacting with Cullen, maintaining a façade of normalcy while knowing the truth about him. The scenes in which Amy and Cullen share quiet moments, knowing that both of them are hiding something from the other, are some of the film's most powerful. The sense of danger is palpable, not because Cullen is physically threatening but because of the psychological toll this deception takes on Amy. The audience is left holding its breath, wondering if Cullen will catch on to her plan before the police can arrest him.

When Cullen is finally arrested, there is no sense of victory. The film doesn't end with a triumphant moment but rather with a quiet sense of relief tinged with sadness. Amy has done the right thing, but it has come at a personal cost. Cullen's arrest doesn't bring back the lives he took, nor does it fully rectify the system that allowed him to continue killing for so long. The film ends on a reflective note, leaving audiences to consider the implications of what they've just witnessed.

The Good Nurse is more than just a dramatization of a true crime story; it's a deeply human film that explores the complexities of morality, trust, and institutional accountability. Jessica Chastain and Eddie Redmayne deliver outstanding performances that bring these real-life figures to life with empathy and nuance. The film's quiet, deliberate pacing allows the story to unfold in a way that feels both authentic and emotionally resonant, drawing the audience into the moral and ethical dilemmas faced by its characters.

Ultimately, The Good Nurse is a film about choices—the choices made by Charles Cullen, by the hospitals that employed him, and by Amy Loughren. It's about the consequences of those choices and the profound impact they have on the lives of others. While Cullen's crimes are the driving force of the narrative, it is Amy's story that lingers. Her courage, compassion, and unwavering sense of duty serve as a reminder that even in the darkest of circumstances, there are those who will stand up for what is right, no matter the cost.

Chapter Two

Charles Cullen—The Angel of Death

Charles Cullen's story is one of the most unsettling and disturbing cases of serial murder in modern history. As a seemingly unremarkable nurse working in hospitals and healthcare facilities across New Jersey and Pennsylvania, he gained the trust of his colleagues and patients. Yet, beneath the surface of his calm and professional demeanor lurked a man responsible for the deaths of hundreds of innocent lives. His ability to abuse his position as a medical worker was not only a reflection of his cunning but also of the systemic failures that allowed him to continue unchecked for nearly two decades.

Charles Edmund Cullen was born on February 22, 1960, in West Orange, New Jersey. He was the youngest of eight children in a working-class family. His father passed away when he was just seven months old, leaving his mother, Florence Cullen, to raise the family on her own. However, life dealt another blow when Cullen was 17 years old—his mother died in a car accident. This loss had a profound effect on him, leaving him with deep emotional scars that he would carry for the rest of his life. His mother's death seemed to be the catalyst for a downward spiral of mental health struggles that would manifest in disturbing ways in the years to come.

After his mother's death, Cullen joined the U.S. Navy, where his emotional instability became increasingly evident. He was assigned to the submarine corps, a prestigious division of the Navy, but his time in the service was marked by erratic behavior. Cullen made several suicide attempts during his naval career, including an incident where he was found seated at the missile controls of his submarine wearing a surgical mask, gloves, and a hospital gown. This bizarre and unsettling episode led to his removal from the submarine corps and eventual discharge from the Navy in 1984. Despite these clear signs of psychological distress, Cullen managed to continue his life outside the military.

After his discharge, Cullen sought stability and purpose in the medical field. He enrolled in the Mountainside Hospital School of Nursing in Montclair, New Jersey, and graduated in 1986. His choice to enter nursing may have seemed altruistic on the surface, but it was within this profession that his deadly impulses would begin to manifest. Cullen's first known victim was at St. Barnabas Medical Center in Livingston, New Jersey, in 1988. He had started working in the burn unit at the hospital, and it was there that he began tampering with intravenous fluid bags. Cullen would inject lethal doses of medications, such as digoxin, insulin, and epinephrine, into the IV bags, which were later administered to patients. These substances, particularly digoxin, a medication used to treat heart conditions, could cause fatal heart arrhythmias if given in excessive amounts. Many of Cullen's early victims were elderly and already seriously ill, making it difficult for anyone to suspect foul play.

Cullen's method was subtle and insidious, allowing him to evade detection for years. By using medications that were easily accessible to nurses and by targeting patients who were already vulnerable, Cullen could hide his crimes behind the guise of medical complications. Hospitals, unfortunately, did not have robust systems in place to track medication discrepancies or unusual patient deaths at the time, which gave Cullen the perfect cover for his deadly activities. However, in 1992, suspicions began to arise at St. Barnabas Medical Center when the hospital noticed an increase in patient deaths and found that IV bags had been tampered with. Rather than launch a full investigation or involve the police, the hospital quietly asked Cullen to resign. This practice of avoiding public scandal would become a recurring theme in Cullen's career, as hospital after hospital failed to take decisive action to stop him.

After leaving St. Barnabas, Cullen moved to Warren Hospital in Phillipsburg, New Jersey, where his killing spree continued. In 1993, he administered a fatal dose of digoxin to an elderly woman named Helen Dean, who was recovering from breast cancer surgery. Her son, Larry Dean, later testified that he had seen Cullen enter his mother's room moments before her sudden and unexpected death. Despite Larry Dean's suspicions and the fact that his mother had been in stable condition before the injection, the hospital took no action against Cullen. Once again, a deadly act of negligence went unnoticed.

By 1998, Cullen had moved to another facility, this time the prestigious Morristown Memorial Hospital in New Jersey. Over the next five years, Cullen continued to kill patients with impunity. He worked at a succession of hospitals, including Liberty Nursing and Rehabilitation Center in Allentown, Pennsylvania, and Easton Hospital, also in Pennsylvania. Each time, Cullen managed to evade suspicion, either by resigning quietly or being transferred to another facility without any formal investigation. It wasn't until 2002, when he began working at Somerset Medical Center in Somerville, New Jersey, that his actions would finally begin to catch up with him.

Somerset Medical Center proved to be a turning point in Cullen's deadly career. By this time, he had become emboldened, killing more frequently and with less caution. Hospital staff noticed an alarming spike in patient deaths, and an internal investigation revealed irregularities in medication logs. Specifically, it was found that patients were receiving lethal doses of digoxin, insulin, and other drugs that had not been prescribed. Yet, even with this mounting evidence, the hospital delayed taking action for fear of lawsuits and damaging its reputation.

In June 2003, the hospital finally contacted the New Jersey Poison Information and Education System (NJPIES), which advised them to report the suspicious deaths to the authorities. However, it wasn't until Amy Loughren, a fellow nurse and colleague of Cullen, began her own investigation that things took a decisive turn. Loughren, who had worked closely with Cullen, had never suspected him of any wrongdoing. But when she was asked to review patient charts, she quickly noticed patterns of drug tampering that pointed directly to Cullen. Shocked and horrified by what she discovered, Loughren made the courageous decision to cooperate with law enforcement to bring him to justice.

In December 2003, Cullen was finally arrested after Loughren agreed to wear a wire during a conversation with him. Her bravery in confronting her former friend and colleague helped police gather the evidence they needed to charge Cullen with multiple counts of murder and attempted murder. During his interrogation, Cullen was evasive and uncooperative, but he eventually confessed to killing around 40 patients over a 16-year period. However, investigators believe the real number of his victims could be as high as 400, making him one of the most prolific serial killers in American history.

On March 2, 2006, Charles Cullen was sentenced to 18 consecutive life sentences without the possibility of parole. He remains incarcerated to this day. Cullen's case prompted widespread calls for reform in the healthcare industry. Hospitals faced intense scrutiny for their role in allowing Cullen to continue his killing spree for so long. The practice of quietly dismissing employees suspected of misconduct, rather than conducting thorough investigations, came under particular fire. In response, many hospitals implemented stricter protocols for monitoring medication usage and tracking suspicious patient deaths. Cullen's crimes also highlighted the need for greater protections for whistleblowers, like Amy Loughren, who played a crucial role in ending his reign of terror.

The legacy of Charles Cullen's crimes is a haunting reminder of the vulnerabilities within the healthcare system. He exploited the very institutions designed to protect and heal, using his position of trust to carry out his deadly agenda. For nearly two decades, Cullen's crimes went undetected, not because he was particularly skilled at hiding them, but because the system was ill-equipped to confront the possibility that one of its own could be capable of such horrific acts.

For the families of Cullen's victims, the pain and uncertainty continue to this day. Many will never know for sure whether their loved ones were among those killed by Cullen, as the true scope of his crimes may never be fully uncovered. His case stands as a dark chapter in the history of American healthcare, one that underscores the importance of vigilance, accountability, and the courage to confront evil, even when it hides in plain sight.

Chapter Three

The Hospitals' Dark Secret

In *The Good Nurse*, one of the most unsettling elements is how Charles Cullen, a nurse responsible for the deaths of dozens, potentially hundreds, of patients, was able to continue his actions over nearly two decades without being stopped. Cullen worked at multiple hospitals across New Jersey and Pennsylvania from the late 1980s through 2003, leaving a trail of patient deaths in his wake. The movie and real-life events expose a dark secret: hospitals that employed Cullen were aware of suspicious deaths occurring during his shifts but chose not to act, prioritizing their reputations over patient safety. The timeline of Cullen's killings and the hospitals' inaction is a disturbing study in institutional failure.

Charles Cullen's career in nursing began in 1987 when he graduated from the Mountainside Hospital School of Nursing in Montclair, New Jersey. His first known position was at Saint Barnabas Medical Center in Livingston, New Jersey. By 1988, Cullen's behavior had already raised suspicions. The first notable incident occurred in 1991, when Cullen was working in the hospital's burn unit. After a spate of patient deaths under mysterious circumstances, an internal investigation was conducted, and it was determined that Cullen had tampered with intravenous (IV) bags, adding lethal doses of insulin. However, instead of confronting Cullen or reporting him to the authorities, Saint

Barnabas quietly allowed him to resign. This decision set a dangerous precedent for the next decade.

The practice of "quiet dismissal" that Saint Barnabas employed is at the heart of the hospitals' dark secret. Rather than report Cullen's suspicious actions to law enforcement or health regulators, the hospital chose to let him leave without a formal investigation. This allowed Cullen to move on to other hospitals, taking with him the knowledge that he could kill without consequence. The reasoning behind Saint Barnabas' decision was clear: to avoid lawsuits and a public scandal that would damage their reputation. The hospital had seen enough red flags but was more concerned with preserving its own image than protecting future patients.

After leaving Saint Barnabas in 1992, Cullen found employment at Warren Hospital in Phillipsburg, New Jersey. It was here that Cullen's methods became even more refined. He began administering lethal doses of digoxin, a heart medication, to patients who were often critically ill. Digoxin was a common medication in hospitals, and an overdose could easily be written off as a mistake or a result of the patient's underlying condition. Over the next few years, the number of unexplained deaths at Warren Hospital grew, but the hospital's administrators did little to investigate.

In one disturbing case in 1993, a patient at Warren Hospital claimed that Cullen had injected her with a lethal substance while she was recovering from heart surgery. The patient survived and reported the incident to hospital officials, but her claim was dismissed as a delusion. Rather than dig deeper into the patient's complaint, Warren Hospital ignored it. The hospital's reluctance to take action, even in the face of direct accusations from a patient, highlighted the broader systemic failure. Hospitals were more focused on minimizing risk and avoiding bad publicity than in thoroughly investigating the behavior of their staff.

Cullen continued working at Warren Hospital until 1996, when he was quietly dismissed again after a series of patient deaths. Yet, no action was taken beyond his departure, allowing him to move on to Hunterdon Medical Center in Flemington, New Jersey. At Hunterdon, Cullen's pattern continued: patients who were not expected to die suddenly succumbed to cardiac arrest after receiving lethal injections of medications. The deaths went largely unexamined, with hospital officials failing to raise alarms about the growing number of fatalities linked to Cullen's shifts.

By the late 1990s, Cullen's actions were beginning to draw more attention, but the healthcare system's protective shield still remained intact. In 1998, Cullen moved to Liberty Nursing and Rehabilitation Center in Allentown, Pennsylvania, where he was responsible for administering medications to elderly patients. It was here that he caused the death of a patient through an insulin overdose, but again, the hospital took no formal action other than allowing Cullen to leave quietly. The lack of communication between hospitals allowed him to continue his deadly career, as no one reported his suspicious behavior to authorities or other healthcare institutions.

The events that unfolded at Somerset Medical Center in Somerville, New Jersey, where Cullen worked from 2002 until his arrest in 2003, finally brought his reign of terror to an end. However, the failure of the hospital system to act sooner is what stands out as the most egregious example of institutional neglect. At Somerset, Cullen killed at least 13 patients using lethal doses of medications like digoxin and insulin.

Despite a significant increase in patient deaths, hospital administrators were slow to investigate, and when they did, their findings were suppressed out of fear of liability.

In 2002, pharmacists at Somerset Medical Center noticed an unusual number of patients suffering from cardiac arrest, particularly those who had received digoxin. Pharmacist William Korsh raised concerns to the hospital administration, but his warnings were initially ignored. It wasn't until months later, in early 2003, that the hospital launched an internal investigation into Cullen's activities. Even then, rather than report their findings to the authorities immediately, Somerset Medical Center attempted to manage the situation internally. The fear of legal repercussions once again outweighed the hospital's duty to protect its patients.

It wasn't until October 2003 that Somerset Medical Center finally contacted law enforcement, after several more patients died under suspicious circumstances. By this point, Cullen's body count had risen dramatically, and the hospital's inaction had cost many lives. When the investigation into Cullen's actions began, it quickly became clear that his killing spree had gone unchecked for far too long. He was arrested in December 2003 and later confessed to killing at least 40 patients, though experts believe the real number could be closer to 400.

The hospitals' dark secret wasn't just their failure to act but their active participation in covering up the crimes. Each hospital that Cullen worked at had the opportunity to stop him, but they chose not to. Whether it was the quiet dismissal from Saint Barnabas, the ignored patient complaint at Warren Hospital, or the delayed response at Somerset Medical Center, the healthcare institutions that employed Cullen failed to prioritize patient safety over their own financial and legal concerns.

This dark truth about the healthcare system is not unique to Cullen's case. Many institutions are more concerned with preserving their reputations than with thoroughly investigating and addressing problems within their walls. In the case of Cullen, this fear of scandal allowed a serial killer to operate with impunity for years, claiming the lives of countless vulnerable patients.

The 2003 arrest and subsequent trial of Charles Cullen brought to light these failures and led to significant changes in hospital policies, including stronger reporting requirements and whistleblower protections. However, the damage had already been done. Cullen was sentenced to life in prison without the possibility of parole, but for the families of his victims, the knowledge that their loved ones' deaths could have been prevented was a bitter pill to swallow.

The real tragedy of Cullen's story is that it was entirely preventable. If even one of the hospitals that employed him had chosen to report his behavior to law enforcement or take decisive action, many lives could have been saved. Instead, they chose the path of least resistance, quietly dismissing him and passing the problem along to the next institution. This culture of secrecy and self-preservation is at the heart of *The Good Nurse* and remains a haunting reminder of the moral compromises that can occur when institutions prioritize their own survival over the safety of the people they are meant to protect.

Cullen's crimes and the hospitals' failure to act serve as a grim warning about the dangers of institutional complacency. While improvements have been made in the years since his arrest, the case of Charles Cullen remains a stark reminder that accountability in the healthcare system is not just a matter of professional ethics—it is a matter of life and death.

Chapter Four

Amy Loughren—The Hero Nurse

Amy Loughren's journey to becoming *The Good Nurse* is one of moral courage, emotional resilience, and a commitment to justice. Born in the 1960s, Amy pursued a career in nursing, a profession that perfectly matched her compassionate nature and desire to help those in need. By the early 2000s, Amy was working long hours as a critical care nurse at Somerset Medical Center in New Jersey, a position that was both physically and emotionally demanding. She was a single mother, raising two daughters while managing the stress and rigors of working in an Intensive Care Unit (ICU). Her daily life was a balancing act between saving lives and ensuring she provided for her family, often leaving her utterly exhausted. It was in this environment that Amy formed a close friendship with fellow nurse Charles Cullen.

In November 2002, Charles Cullen was hired at Somerset Medical Center, having already worked at several hospitals across New Jersey and Pennsylvania. Cullen and Amy worked the night shift together in the ICU, where they bonded over the shared pressures of their profession. Amy found Cullen to be kind, calm, and trustworthy—a seemingly perfect colleague. Cullen was attentive to patients, often going above and beyond in providing care, and he quickly became one of Amy's closest friends at the hospital. They would confide in one another about their personal lives and the struggles they faced, with Amy frequently praising Cullen's dedication to his work.

Yet, beneath Cullen's friendly exterior lay a horrifying secret. Unbeknownst to Amy, Cullen was secretly murdering patients by administering lethal doses of medications like insulin and digoxin, drugs that would send patients into sudden, deadly heart failure. Over the course of his 16-year career, Cullen had worked at nine different hospitals, and although he had been suspected of wrongdoing at several of them, no institution had ever fully investigated him. Hospital administrators were more concerned about the potential for lawsuits than patient safety and often quietly let him go without alerting authorities.

Cullen's crimes at Somerset Medical Center began to surface in mid-2003. A string of suspicious deaths prompted hospital administrators to launch an internal review, and eventually, the New Jersey Poison Control Center became involved. By October 2003, Cullen's activities had come under intense scrutiny, and the hospital reported their suspicions to the New Jersey Department of Health and law enforcement. But without concrete evidence, they were unable to take immediate action. It was at this point that detectives reached out to Amy Loughren, who was still working alongside Cullen, completely unaware of his deadly actions.

In December 2003, Amy was approached by detectives Danny Baldwin and Tim Braun. They informed her that Cullen was a suspect in a series of patient deaths and asked for her help. The request devastated Amy. Cullen had been her friend, a person she trusted implicitly. But as the detectives laid out the evidence they had gathered, including drug use anomalies in patient records and unusual death patterns, Amy began to see the cracks in Cullen's façade. She was left to grapple with the horrifying realization that her colleague and friend could be a serial killer.

Initially, Amy struggled to believe the allegations. It seemed impossible that someone as kind and caring as Cullen could be capable of such atrocities. Yet, as she reviewed the medical records that the detectives provided, Amy's doubt turned into a sickening certainty. She recognized that many of the patients who had died had received medications that they should not have been given, often at times when Cullen was on duty. One particularly jarring case was that of a patient who had been recovering well, only to suddenly die after receiving a fatal dose of digoxin. Amy began to notice a pattern—Cullen had been present for nearly every suspicious death.

Amy's internal turmoil was immense. She had to continue working alongside Cullen, pretending that everything was normal while secretly assisting the detectives in building a case against him. She was terrified that if Cullen realized she was helping the police, she or her children could be in danger. Yet, Amy knew that she had a moral obligation to help stop Cullen before he could kill more patients. Her decision to cooperate with law enforcement was not an easy one, but it was necessary.

As the investigation continued, the detectives asked Amy to wear a wire and confront Cullen. This request marked the turning point in Amy's journey from a nurse caught in the crossfire to a hero determined to seek justice. In mid-December 2003, Amy agreed to meet with Cullen at a local diner. The goal was to engage him in a conversation about the deaths at the hospital in the hopes of eliciting a confession or at least enough incriminating information to solidify the case against him.

The meeting was tense, with Amy playing the role of a concerned friend who wanted to understand why their patients were dying. She skillfully navigated the conversation, asking probing questions without arousing Cullen's suspicion. Cullen, for his part, was cryptic but didn't explicitly deny the accusations. Instead, he alluded to feeling trapped and made comments that confirmed Amy's worst fears—he had been killing patients, and he didn't seem to feel any remorse. It was a chilling interaction that left Amy shaken but determined to see the investigation through to the end.

Cullen's arrest came shortly after the diner meeting. On December 14, 2003, he was taken into custody, and in the days that followed, he began to confess to his crimes. Cullen admitted to killing at least 40 patients, though experts believe the actual number could be much higher, potentially as many as 400. His method was simple but effective—he would administer drugs that would either cause a patient's heart to stop or lead to a fatal overdose, often doing so in a way that made the deaths appear natural.

In April 2004, Cullen pleaded guilty to multiple counts of murder. He was sentenced to 11 consecutive life sentences without the possibility of parole, effectively ensuring that he would spend the rest of his life in prison. His sentencing brought some closure to the families of his victims, but the scale of his crimes and the failures of the hospitals where he worked left a lasting scar on the medical community.

For Amy Loughren, Cullen's arrest and conviction marked the end of a deeply traumatic chapter in her life. She had gone from being a nurse caring for patients to a key figure in one of the most shocking healthcare-related criminal cases in modern history. Amy's bravery in confronting Cullen and working with law enforcement cannot be overstated. Without her cooperation, it is possible that Cullen's crimes would have continued unchecked for even longer.

After Cullen's conviction, Amy Loughren spoke publicly about the emotional toll the experience had taken on her. She had been forced to reconcile the image of Charles Cullen, the friend she thought she knew, with the reality of Charles Cullen, the serial killer who had used his position of trust to murder innocent people. Amy also faced the difficult task of explaining the situation to her children, who had known Cullen as a family friend. Despite the personal anguish she endured, Amy has expressed relief that she was able to help bring Cullen to justice, knowing that her actions saved countless lives.

The legacy of Amy Loughren's heroism lives on, not only in the lives she helped save but in the broader conversation about patient safety and accountability in healthcare. Her story highlights the importance of speaking up when something seems wrong, even in environments where loyalty to colleagues can sometimes overshadow moral responsibility. Amy's courage in stepping forward, despite the personal risk, serves as a powerful reminder that individuals can make a difference, even in the face of overwhelming odds.

The Good Nurse captures the essence of Amy Loughren's extraordinary journey. While the film dramatizes certain elements of the story, it remains true to the emotional heart of Amy's experience—her deep sense of duty to her patients, her inner conflict over her friendship with Cullen, and her ultimate decision to risk everything to stop him. Amy Loughren didn't set out to be a hero, but her actions helped bring one of the most prolific serial killers in modern history to justice. In doing so, she proved that even in the darkest of times, there is light to be found in the choices we make to protect others.

Chapter Five

Unmasking the Monster

Charles Cullen, a registered nurse, had built a career spanning 16 years across several hospitals in New Jersey and Pennsylvania. During this time, he became one of the most prolific serial killers in American history, responsible for the deaths of dozens, perhaps hundreds, of patients. Cullen's killings were deliberate, and his ability to evade detection for so long stemmed from institutional failures, as hospitals were more concerned with avoiding lawsuits than protecting their patients. By the time the true extent of his crimes came to light in 2003, Cullen had already claimed an unimaginable number of lives. What followed was a tense investigation, one that would rely heavily on the courage of a single nurse, Amy Loughren, to bring Cullen to justice.

The story of Charles Cullen's eventual unmasking began in September 2002, at Somerset Medical Center in Somerville, New Jersey. By this point in his career, Cullen had already worked at nine different hospitals, and each time, suspicious patient deaths followed in his wake. Despite the red flags, Cullen was often allowed to resign or was quietly dismissed without any criminal investigations. This allowed him to continue his deadly spree, as his next employer would be none the wiser to his actions. Somerset was no different—until a series of unexpected deaths caught the attention of hospital administrators.

In June 2003, the first significant warning sign emerged when a patient named Florian Gall, 68, died unexpectedly after being admitted to Somerset for a heart condition. His death was initially attributed to complications related to his illness. However, when toxicology reports revealed an abnormal amount of digoxin—a heart medication used to strengthen the heartbeat but fatal in large doses—in his system, hospital administrators began to worry. They launched an internal investigation, but it was limited and did not uncover any solid proof of wrongdoing. Meanwhile, patients continued to die under suspicious circumstances.

By the summer of 2003, Amy Loughren, a fellow nurse at Somerset Medical Center, had been working alongside Charles Cullen for nearly a year. Like many of her colleagues, she initially saw him as a quiet, dedicated nurse who was always willing to help others. Loughren, a single mother of two, was battling health issues of her own, including cardiomyopathy, which caused her heart to weaken. Cullen had often helped her during difficult shifts, offering friendship and support, and in return, she trusted him.

However, that trust would soon be shattered.

In October 2003, Somerset Medical Center reported their growing concerns about Cullen to local authorities. This triggered an investigation by the New Jersey State Police and the Somerset County Prosecutor's Office. Detectives Tim Braun and Danny Baldwin were assigned to the case, and they immediately recognized that something was wrong. Several patients had died unexpectedly, and all of the deaths seemed to have occurred during Cullen's shifts. However, they had no hard evidence to tie Cullen to the deaths. They needed help from someone on the inside.

Enter Amy Loughren. In November 2003, after learning about the police investigation, Loughren was approached by Braun and Baldwin. At first, she couldn't believe what she was hearing. Cullen, her friend and colleague, couldn't possibly be responsible for the deaths of their patients. But as the detectives laid out the evidence—pointing out the suspicious timing of the deaths, the patterns of medication use, and Cullen's troubled history at previous hospitals—Loughren began to doubt her perception of him.

Determined to find the truth, Amy agreed to help the detectives. She started looking more closely at Cullen's behavior. What she found was chilling. Patients who had been stable would suddenly crash and die during Cullen's shifts. Medical charts showed that medications like digoxin, insulin, and epinephrine—drugs that could be lethal in the wrong doses—were being administered to patients without any medical justification. The more Amy observed, the clearer it became: Cullen was deliberately killing patients.

One particular case stood out. On July 14, 2003, a woman named Reverend Gall died at Somerset

Medical Center under suspicious circumstances. The toxicology reports revealed a lethal level of digoxin in her system, a drug she had never been prescribed. It was around this time that hospital administrators, after consulting with poison control experts, suspected that a member of their staff was intentionally harming patients. This prompted the hospital to alert the authorities, which led to the eventual involvement of Amy Loughren.

In the weeks that followed, Amy provided critical information to the police. She monitored Cullen's interactions with patients and collected details on medication usage, particularly focusing on drugs like digoxin. She even combed through medical records, discovering that several patients had been given these medications despite not having prescriptions for them. With Amy's help, the detectives began to build a solid case against Cullen.

In December 2003, Amy was asked to do the unthinkable: confront Cullen. Detectives needed her to engage him in conversation, to get him to open up about the deaths. It was a dangerous move, one that could have backfired if Cullen had suspected anything. Nevertheless, Amy agreed. On December 12, 2003, she met with Cullen at a local diner. The tension was palpable. Amy had to act as though nothing was wrong, as though she hadn't discovered the horrifying truth about her friend.

During their conversation, Amy carefully steered the discussion toward the patient deaths. She mentioned that the police were investigating the hospital and suggested that perhaps medication errors had been made. Cullen's response was chilling. Instead of denying the possibility, he seemed to acknowledge that mistakes could have been made. He didn't confess outright, but his evasive answers and lack of surprise made it clear to Amy that he was guilty. That night, as she walked out of the diner, Amy knew that her suspicions had been confirmed.

With this interaction, the police finally had enough to arrest Charles Cullen. On December 14, 2003, Cullen was taken into custody. However, even in jail, he remained silent, refusing to admit to his crimes. The detectives knew that they needed a confession to secure a conviction, and once again, they turned to Amy for help. In a final act of courage, Amy visited Cullen in prison. She pleaded with him to tell the truth, not for her sake, but for the families of his victims. It was during this emotional conversation that Cullen finally cracked. He confessed to killing patients but claimed he couldn't remember the exact number. Later, Cullen would tell police that he had killed as many as 40 patients, though experts believe the true number may be closer to 400.

On March 2, 2006, Charles Cullen was sentenced to 11 consecutive life terms in prison without the possibility of parole. He remains incarcerated to this day. His case stands as one of the most horrifying examples of medical professionals abusing their position of trust to commit murder. Despite the enormous tragedy, it was Amy Loughren's bravery that ultimately led to Cullen's downfall. Her willingness to confront the monster in her midst, to risk her safety and career to stop him, makes her the true hero of this story.

In the years following Cullen's conviction, hospitals across the United States were forced to re-examine their practices. Cullen's ability to move from hospital to hospital without being detected exposed a deep flaw in the healthcare system's accountability mechanisms. Many hospitals instituted stricter protocols for monitoring staff and medication use, but for the families of Cullen's victims, these reforms came too late.

Amy Loughren has since spoken publicly about her role in bringing Cullen to justice. She continues to work as a nurse, though the emotional toll of the investigation has left its mark on her. In interviews, she has described the guilt she felt after discovering that Cullen had been killing patients right under her nose. But despite the trauma, Amy remains proud of her actions. She helped to stop one of the most prolific serial killers in history, and for that, she will always be remembered as the good nurse who unmasked the monster.

Chapter Six

Comparing the Movie to Reality

The Good Nurse, a film adaptation of Charles Graeber's nonfiction book, takes the chilling true story of Charles Cullen, a nurse who became one of the most prolific serial killers in American history, and transforms it into a gripping cinematic experience. The movie does an exceptional job of maintaining the gravity of the real-life events, while still making some necessary narrative adjustments for dramatic effect. As with most films based on true stories, The Good Nurse balances fact with fiction, aiming to convey the emotional weight of the story while navigating the complexities of real-world events.

The portrayal of Charles Cullen in the movie, played with eerie precision by Eddie Redmayne, is one of the most striking aspects of the adaptation. Cullen was a man who, on the surface, seemed to blend into his environment. He worked quietly, efficiently, and with an air of normalcy that allowed him to move between hospitals, undetected as his crimes mounted. In reality, Cullen's outward demeanor was integral to his ability to carry out these murders. The film captures this element of Cullen's personality effectively, but it also amplifies some of his behaviors to make him a more visibly unsettling figure. In the movie, there are moments of tension where Cullen's character exudes an overt sense of danger, perhaps more than Cullen might have shown in real life. These moments serve the film's need to create suspense, but they also depart slightly from the accounts of Cullen being more quietly manipulative and emotionally complex.

Jessica Chastain's portrayal of Amy Loughren, the nurse who helped bring Cullen to justice, is deeply empathetic and humanizing. In real life, Loughren was a single mother dealing with her own health struggles, working long hours while managing a challenging personal life. The film mirrors much of this reality, portraying her as overworked and overwhelmed, but it does condense some aspects of her journey. In real life, Loughren's realization of Cullen's crimes wasn't as sudden as it is depicted in the film. The movie compresses her investigation into a more cinematic timeline, with dramatic confrontations and quick revelations. This makes for an intense narrative but simplifies the slower, more methodical process that Loughren actually went through. She had suspicions, but the realization of the full extent of Cullen's actions came more gradually, as she pieced together the anomalies in his patient charts over time.

In one of the movie's most heart-pounding scenes, Amy confronts Cullen in a restaurant, trying to draw out a confession while working with the police. This confrontation adds a layer of suspense and drama that heightens the film's emotional stakes. However, such a scene never took place in reality. While Loughren did play a crucial role in gathering evidence and cooperating with law enforcement, much of her involvement happened behind the scenes. She wore a wire and worked closely with the police, but there was no climactic showdown. This fictionalized encounter is an example of the filmmakers taking creative liberties to amplify the tension and create a cinematic moment that leaves the audience on edge.

Another important divergence between the movie and the real story is the portrayal of the hospital system's response to Cullen's actions. In the film, hospitals appear to be dismissive and complicit, protecting their reputations at the cost of patient safety. This portrayal, while not inaccurate, simplifies the reality of the institutional failures that allowed Cullen to continue his killing spree across multiple healthcare facilities. In reality, the hospital administrators did not outright shield Cullen with malicious intent, but they also did not act with the urgency or transparency necessary to prevent further deaths. Many hospitals quietly dismissed Cullen or failed to investigate thoroughly, more concerned with avoiding lawsuits than uncovering the truth. The film captures the frustration and anger of those who sought justice, but it stops short of fully unpacking the complexities of institutional negligence. It's a subtle distinction, but one that reflects the difference between storytelling for impact and the more intricate realities of bureaucracy and systemic failure.

One of the film's most emotionally charged elements is the relationship between Amy Loughren and Charles Cullen. The movie leans heavily into the tension between their friendship and the eventual betrayal that Amy feels as she uncovers the truth. In real life, Loughren did have a professional relationship with Cullen, but the film enhances their bond to create more emotional depth. This isn't to say that Loughren wasn't devastated by her discoveries—she was. But the film intensifies their connection to build a stronger emotional arc, which allows the audience to more acutely feel Amy's internal struggle as she grapples with Cullen's horrifying actions. This decision serves the film's narrative goals, even if it bends the truth slightly for dramatic effect.

Another area where The Good Nurse takes creative liberties is in the way it depicts Cullen's crimes. The movie streamlines the timeline of his killings, giving the impression that his actions were more concentrated in a specific period. In reality, Cullen's killing spree spanned over 16 years and involved multiple hospitals in different states. The film, by necessity, compresses this timeline to maintain a cohesive narrative. It focuses on the period when Amy Loughren became involved, using her perspective as the lens through which the audience views the unfolding events. This decision not only sharpens the focus of the story but also ensures that the film remains tightly paced, preventing it from becoming bogged down in the more protracted real-life timeline of Cullen's crimes.

One of the more subtle yet impactful changes in the film is the depiction of Cullen's method of killing. In real life, Cullen used digoxin, insulin, and other medications to induce fatal heart attacks in his victims. The film stays true to this detail, but it doesn't dwell too heavily on the technicalities of his methods. Instead, it focuses on the emotional aftermath of the deaths and the growing suspicions surrounding Cullen. This approach allows the film to maintain a balance between the procedural elements of the story and the human toll of Cullen's actions. While the real-life investigation would have involved more complex medical analysis and forensic work, the movie streamlines these aspects to keep the story accessible and emotionally engaging for the audience.

What The Good Nurse does exceptionally well is capturing the moral dilemma at the heart of the story. Amy Loughren is portrayed as a nurse who is deeply compassionate and committed to her patients, but she is also someone who is placed in an almost unbearable situation—having to reconcile her professional responsibilities with the horrifying realization that her friend and colleague is a murderer. This internal conflict is central to both the movie and the real-life story. In reality, Loughren was torn between her loyalty to her profession, her patients, and her desire to protect the vulnerable, and the film captures this emotional struggle with great sensitivity. Even though certain aspects of her story are dramatized for effect, the core of her character remains intact.

Chapter Seven

The Impact of the True Story

The Good Nurse is not merely a compelling true crime thriller, but a poignant reflection on a system that failed to protect its most vulnerable—patients who trusted hospitals with their lives. As the film takes viewers through the unsettling journey of Charles Cullen's heinous acts and the heroism of Amy Loughren, the aftermath of these real-life events is equally significant. The chilling reality of Cullen's crimes left a lasting mark not only on the victims' families but on the entire healthcare industry. The lessons learned from this tragedy are profound, affecting both medical institutions and individuals who work within them.

After Cullen's arrest, the spotlight turned to the glaring institutional failures that allowed him to continue his killing spree for so many years. Hospitals, places meant to provide healing and care, became enablers through their inaction and prioritization of reputation over patient safety. This was the most damning realization that emerged from Cullen's case: numerous hospitals had suspected his involvement in patient deaths, but instead of investigating thoroughly or alerting authorities, they quietly dismissed him, allowing him to move on to the next institution. In doing so, they transferred a grave threat to another facility, another set of patients, and another unsuspecting staff, ultimately prolonging Cullen's ability to commit his atrocities.

This practice, known as "passing the trash," was shockingly prevalent in Cullen's case. Each hospital's reluctance to involve law enforcement out of fear of litigation or damage to their public image played a critical role in prolonging the carnage. The fallout from this realization led to significant pressure on healthcare systems to reassess their priorities. It became evident that the lack of transparency and accountability in the healthcare industry had to change if such events were to be prevented in the future.

In the immediate aftermath, there were calls for systemic reforms within the medical community. Hospital policies were scrutinized, and procedures around reporting suspicious activity or staff misconduct were re-examined. One of the key reforms was the implementation of more stringent background checks for medical staff. While Cullen had been licensed and credentialed as a nurse, there had been several red flags in his career, including unusual patient deaths and staff complaints. However, these warning signs were largely ignored or dismissed due to the lack of a cohesive system for tracking such incidents across hospitals. The creation of a national database that tracks healthcare workers' employment histories, disciplinary actions, and any suspicious behavior became one of the most important outcomes of the Cullen case. This database now helps hospitals identify problematic employees, preventing them from simply moving to another institution without consequence.

The Cullen case also highlighted the crucial role of whistleblowers in safeguarding patients' well-being. Amy Loughren, the nurse who worked closely with Cullen and ultimately helped the police bring him to justice, exemplifies the importance of speaking up, even when doing so carries personal and professional risks. In the film, The Good Nurse, Amy's courage is portrayed not just as an act of moral responsibility, but as one rooted in deep compassion for her patients and a belief that healthcare workers have a duty to protect those in their care. In real life, Amy's bravery set a powerful precedent for others in the medical field, encouraging healthcare professionals to trust their instincts and report suspicious behavior, even if it means going against powerful institutions.

Following the exposure of Cullen's crimes, hospitals and healthcare organizations began to prioritize the protection and support of whistleblowers. Policies were put in place to shield individuals who report unethical or dangerous behavior from retaliation, making it safer for medical workers to come forward. This shift represented a broader cultural change within the healthcare industry, one where patient safety and ethical responsibility became the guiding principles. Amy Loughren's role in the Cullen case was a reminder that healthcare workers are often the last line of defense when systems fail, and their voices must be heard and protected.

However, the aftermath of Cullen's crimes was not limited to policy changes within the medical community. The families of his victims were left grappling with an immense sense of loss and betrayal. These families had trusted hospitals to provide the best care for their loved ones, only to discover that the very institutions meant to heal had played a role in their deaths. The emotional toll on these families cannot be overstated. Many of them became advocates for hospital transparency and accountability, determined to ensure that no other family would have to experience the same heartbreak. Their efforts helped drive legislative changes, leading to the passage of laws aimed at increasing transparency in healthcare and holding hospitals accountable for their staff's actions.

One of the most significant outcomes of the Cullen case was the public's heightened awareness of the need for oversight in the healthcare system. Patients and their families became more vigilant, asking more questions about the care they were receiving and the backgrounds of the medical professionals they were entrusting with their lives. This shift in patient behavior created a new dynamic in the healthcare system, where institutions had to be more transparent and responsive to concerns about safety and ethical practices. No longer could hospitals operate under a veil of secrecy; the public demanded accountability.

The release of The Good Nurse further amplified this awareness, bringing Cullen's story to a global audience and reigniting discussions about healthcare safety. The film, while a dramatization of real events, served as a powerful reminder of the dangers of complacency within medical institutions. Audiences were confronted with the harsh reality that healthcare, an industry built on trust, could be manipulated by individuals with nefarious intentions, and that institutions must do more to protect their patients. The film also underscored the importance of moral courage, as exemplified by Amy Loughren's decision to stand up for what was right, despite the risks involved.

In the years following Cullen's arrest, Amy Loughren has become an enduring symbol of integrity and bravery in the healthcare field. She has spoken publicly about her experiences and the emotional toll of discovering that her friend and colleague was responsible for so many deaths. Her story serves as a reminder of the ethical dilemmas that healthcare workers may face and the profound responsibility they carry in protecting their patients. Amy's legacy is one of compassion, resilience, and a commitment to doing what is right, even in the face of overwhelming odds.

The lessons learned from The Good Nurse are not limited to the healthcare industry. They extend to any institution where individuals are entrusted with the well-being of others. The Cullen case is a stark reminder that transparency, accountability, and ethical responsibility must be at the forefront of any organization's mission. The consequences of ignoring red flags, prioritizing reputation over safety, and failing to support whistleblowers can be catastrophic.

In conclusion, The Good Nurse is not just a film about a serial killer—it is a reflection on the systemic failures that allowed Charles Cullen to continue his killing spree for years. The aftermath of this case has led to significant reforms in the healthcare industry, from improved background checks and whistleblower protections to greater transparency and accountability. Amy Loughren's courage in the face of unimaginable circumstances has left a lasting impact, inspiring others in the medical field to prioritize patient safety above all else. The lessons learned from Cullen's crimes serve as a powerful reminder that institutions must always act in the best interest of those they are meant to protect, and that individual acts of bravery can make all the difference in bringing justice to light.

www.ingramcontent.com/pod-product-compliance
Lightning Source LLC
LaVergne TN
LVHW010558070526
838199LV00063BA/5007